I0866601

"*Find Your Joy Here* is an emotionally intelligent invitation to healing. Lisa Schab guides teens with warmth, clarity, and creativity, offering not just a break from sadness, but a real way through it. This isn't just a journal; it's a brain-wise, heart-forward tool for resilience."

—**MELANIE MCNALLY, PsyD**, clinical psychologist, White House panelist for teen mental health, and author of *The Emotionally Intelligent Teen*

"This book is an amazing resource to help teens change the channel on negative thought spirals. Easygoing and engaging, readers are invited to play with thoughts, memories, and ideas about joy in a way that feels light, easy, and fun. There is something for everyone in these prompts and activities! A fabulous tool for creating and capturing fun and joy."

—**CHERYL M. BRADSHAW, RP, BEd, MA**, Registered Psychotherapist, TEDx speaker on the topic of consent, and author of *How to Like Yourself*, *The Resilience Workbook for Teens*, and *Real Talk About Sex and Consent*

"*Find Your Joy Here* by Lisa Schab is a compassionate, creative journal that helps teens move through sadness and discover moments of happiness. With engaging, easy-to-follow exercises, it encourages self-expression and reflection, whether used alone or in groups. This welcoming tool invites teens to feel their emotions honestly while gently guiding them toward joy and hope. A powerful, practical tool for supporting teen mental health and emotional well-being."

—**JORI BOWEN, MEd, MA**, educator and principal at Lakes Community High School in Lake Villa, IL

"Finding the intricate balance of celebrating the good in life while recognizing sadness that we experience as humans, Lisa Schab creates a perfect space for adolescents to reflect on their complex lives in her guided journal, *Find Your Joy Here*. She validates kids' emotions by assuring them that what they are feeling is 'normal'—something all adolescents strive to achieve, yet rarely feel. She uses language that kids can easily understand and relate to!"

—**KATHERINE MCNEILL, MEd**, eighth-grade English language arts teacher, and certified reading specialist with eleven years of experience in literacy instruction

"Lisa Schab's latest book is a thoughtful and skillfully crafted journal that gives teens a safe space to explore their emotions, emote, and build lifelong coping skills. As a colleague and longtime referring pediatrician, I've seen how her resources support adolescents in moments of sadness while empowering them to manage their mental health with greater confidence and self-awareness."

—**MICHAEL BAUER, MD, FAAP**, assistant professor of clinical pediatrics at the Northwestern University Feinberg School of Medicine

"*Find Your Joy Here* is another wonderful example of Lisa Schab's ability to speak in a relatable way to teens and preteens. Often, in the therapeutic process, we focus on relaxation and coping skills, but we forget about joy and having fun! This workbook helps readers to focus on the 'glimmers,' and things that bring them joy and silliness in their lives."

—**GERALDINE O'SULLIVAN, LCSW, PPSC**, San Diego County High School Social Worker of the Year in 2022, and author of *The Middle School Survival Guide for Girls*

"*Find Your Joy Here* by Lisa Schab is like a treasure map for navigating both joy and sadness! As a creative arts therapist who loves to think outside the box, I'm always excited to discover new ways to help kids and teens explore their emotions and develop coping skills—ways that feel more like an adventure than a task. This book invites readers to engage with their feelings, find creative ways to embrace both the highs and the lows, and build emotional resilience. If you want to support a teen in discovering the full range of their emotions—joy and sadness alike—this book is an absolute gem!"

—**KATE SHANNON, LCAT, LCPC**, licensed adolescent therapist, and host of the *Creative Therapy Umbrella* podcast

"In Lisa Schab's *Find Your Joy Here*, teens can start a journey to discover and express positive emotions. The journal offers activities that help them navigate and balance both sadness and happiness. I appreciate how the author encourages identifying sources of joy; in today's world, where feelings shift quickly, it's a necessary reminder. As a parent and community leader, I'm thrilled my children and the teens I work with have this resource."

—**KENDRIA VICKERS, MSA**, executive board member of the youth empowerment organization, Prettiest Pearls; and chief financial officer of the STEM education company, Super Noah Super Math

"The title of Lisa's thoughtfully crafted journal is apropos to the experience of interacting with it. *Find Your Joy Here* is a gentle invitation to acknowledge difficult emotions while also using imagination to explore and experience joy in real time. The engaging and often sensory nature of the writing prompts is irresistible: you don't just read them; you *feel* them. Each pen stroke generates new insights and fresh perspectives. Pure magic."

—**TERRI WEBB, LCSW, CPEC**, independent school counselor, executive coach, and psychotherapist in private practice

"Lisa Schab's *Find Your Joy Here* is a delightful, engaging guided journal for teens managing their emotions, and a clever disguise for delivering evidence-based clinical practices and skill building. The prompts run the gamut from silly to introspective, yet Schab manages to keep them light, providing encouragement for even the least artistic among us to participate. A wonderful resource to help teens feel more in control and empowered in their lives!"

—**SUSAN WEINSTEIN, JD**, executive director of Families for Depression Awareness

Find Your Joy Here

A Creative Journal to Help Teens Release Sadness & Depression & Find Moments of Happiness Every Day

Lisa M. Schab, LCSW

INSTANT HELP BOOKS
An Imprint of New Harbinger Publications, Inc.

Publisher's Note

New Harbinger Publications is an employee-owned company.

Instant Help Books
An imprint of New Harbinger Publications, Inc.
5720 Shattuck Avenue
Oakland, CA 94609
www.newharbinger.com

Cover and interior design by Amy Shoup.
Illustrations by Sara Christian.
Acquired by Tesilya Hanauer.

Printed in the United States of America

27 26 25

10 9 8 7 6 5 4 3 2 1 First Printing

This book is dedicated
to every amazing teen
who reads these words!
May you accept your
sadness when it comes
and then allow it to roll
away, leaving a welcoming
open space where you can
celebrate all your joys.

DOOR TO JOY

(Want a little break from sadness? Step inside!)

WELCOME!

MAKE YOURSELF COMFORTABLE!
TAKE A BREATH!

Seriously. Taking a break from sadness starts with taking care of yourself. So, find a place to curl up, lose your shoes, and chill for a bit. This will help you to take in the good news that's just ahead.

First, a question:

Have you ever felt
(or are you feeling right now) . . .

A little down?

A little low?

A little heavy?

A little slow?

A little tired?

A little sad?

A little gloomy?

A little bad?

CIRCLE ANY AND ALL THAT APPLY.

If you circled ANY of the above, you're a normal human! Because sadness and low mood are felt by *every human being* at some point or another.

AND NOW, THE PROMISED GOOD NEWS:

1 <u>Experiencing sadness is *normal*</u>. Everyone feels sad at some time. It may not be your first choice of feelings, but there's nothing wrong with this experience, and there's nothing wrong with you for feeling it!

2 <u>Sadness can actually help us</u> learn about and pay attention to ourselves. When we feel sad, we're reminded of what matters to us, and what gives our life meaning. Sadness is like a signal that can prompt us to take action—to either give ourselves some self-care or make some kind of change.

3 Despite sadness being normal and helpful, it's also normal to need a break from it. That's what this book is for! It gives you the chance to **<u>release some of your sadness</u>** and **<u>shift your focus</u>** for a little while.

4 Releasing some of your sadness and shifting your focus doesn't change what's happening outside of you, but it does help **<u>change what's happening inside of you</u>**. And when you take these two steps, you're giving yourself a break in the moment *and* helping your brain get better at taking breaks in the future.

> The joy we feel has little to do with the circumstances of our lives and everything to do with the focus of our lives.
>
> —RUSSELL M. NELSON

5 The journaling prompts in this book will help you: accept, express, and release sadness; distract you from sadness; use meditation or visualization to bring peace to your body, mind, and spirit; and consciously shift your focus to something joyful.

VERY IMPORTANT NOTE: If your sadness ever starts to feel way too big or overwhelming, or like you can't handle it alone or you don't feel safe, it's time to ask for help! Reach out to someone you trust, or if no one you know is available, call 988 for emotional support or go to the nearest emergency room. People all over the world are ready and waiting to help you.

A FEW NOTES ON THE NATURE OF JOY

You can think of joy as anything that...

- LIFTS YOU UP
- BRIGHTENS YOUR DAY
- makes your heart dance
- MAKES YOUR SOUL SING
- PULLS YOU INTO A SMILE

Finding joy doesn't require some amazing, phenomenal circumstance to occur. Joy can come in "glimmers." We can find it in a ray of sun, a puppy's eyes, or a smile from a special person.

Joy doesn't have to be a roller coaster ~ it can be a bike ride.

Joy doesn't have to be fireworks ~ it can be the glow of a single candle.

> Joy comes to us in moments—ordinary moments. We risk missing out on joy when we get too busy chasing down the extraordinary.
>
> —BRENÉ BROWN

Just as feeling sadness doesn't mean there is nothing to be happy about in your life, experiencing joy doesn't mean you will never feel sadness again.

> **Joy can live beside sorrow. Life is messy, unpredictable, and seldom tied into neat little boxes.**
>
> —JONATHAN VAN NESS

On really cloudy days, you might not be able to see the ball of fire that is our sun, and on really low days when you feel a lot of sadness, you might not be able to see joy anywhere. But when the clouds pass, there is always more sun. When the sadness passes, there is always more joy. The clouds and the sadness are not permanent. This book will give you dozens of ways to get through the clouds and find some joy again.

A FEW TIPS FOR USING THIS BOOK:

1 Think of this book as a space for releasing the sadness you are feeling in the moment and a guide for how to replace the sadness with glimmers of happiness and joy.

2 Only you know what brings you sadness and joy. You are the expert on what feels best as you go through this journal. So, make it yours! Choose the prompts that feel good to you in the moment. Do them in whatever order feels right for you.

3 When the prompts suggest that you write or draw something, *please remember* that this is not an English or art class. Not even close! You don't have to be a good writer or artist to complete a prompt. There's no finished product required. The only goal is to feel better. So let yourself scribble away!

4 Finally, feel free to wiggle the prompt suggestions around to make them fit your personal needs. For example, if it feels better to you, you can write when it says draw, color over words, make a list even if it doesn't direct you to, cut out or color an image if you like it, follow only half the instructions, or whatever else helps release your sadness and bring you joy.

> For in the dew of little things
> the heart finds its morning
> and is refreshed.
>
> —KAHLIL GIBRAN

This is your invitation . . . come in and refresh your heart . . .

> If you carry joy in your heart,
> you can heal any moment.
>
> —CARLOS SANTANA

Show what you can carry within you to keep your heart filled with joy.

EVEN ON A DAY

WHEN IT FEELS LIKE

EVERYTHING IS

GOING WRONG,

THERE IS STILL

SOMETHING

THAT IS

GOING RIGHT.

WHAT IS IT TODAY?

WHAT MAKES ME HAPPY

FOOD ______________________________

COLOR ______________________________

PERSON ______________________________

ANIMAL ______________________________

GAME ______________________________

MONTH ______________________________

MOVIE ______________________________

SONG ______________________________

PLACE ______________________________

RESTAURANT ______________________________

CITY ______________________________

CLASS ______________________________

TIME OF DAY ______________________________

SEASON ______________________________

SMELL ______________________________

BOOK

MEME

BEVERAGE

VIDEO

SPORT

ACTOR

HOBBY

AUTHOR

CLOTHES

JEWELRY

JOKE

TV SHOW

WHAT ELSE? . . .

DRAW OR DESCRIBE THE

THERAPY ANIMAL

YOU'D LIKE TO HELP YOU THROUGH YOUR SADNESS.

Breed? ______________________

Color? ______________________

Size? ______________________

Personality? ______________________

Name? ______________________

How do they feel to touch?

____

IMAGINE AND FEEL THEIR COMFORT NOW.

AFFIRMATIONS FOR JOY

"THE POSSIBILITIES OF ME ARE LIMITLESS."

"MY UNIQUENESS IS MY STRENGTH."

"I AM WHOLE AND COMPLETE JUST AS I AM."

Decorate those you like. Write your own!

"I ACCEPT ALL THE GOOD COMING MY WAY."

"I AM OPEN TO MIRACLES."

"I AM NOT MY PAST."

"THE BEST IS YET TO COME."

YOU WAKE UP TO AN UNEXPECTED

DAY OFF SCHOOL

And all your homework is done!

Describe everything you do on your fabulous day of freedom.

FIND PHOTOS THAT BRING YOU JOY. TAPE THEM IN THESE FRAMES!

You have a right to your **SAD** feelings. Put them in here.

Now take a moment to separate yourself from them.

Draw yourself here.

Breathe peacefully and feel the separation.

Gratitude creates a path to

Look at your WHOLE life . . . What are you grateful for today?
(people, places, events, situations, things, talents, and??)

JOY

Write about a memory that makes you smile from ear to ear . . .

WRITE THE LYRICS TO A **SAD** SONG HERE.

Sing it or play it over and over until all your sadness has left you and been blown out into the stars.

BACK SCRATCH

COOL WATER SPLASH

FOOT RUB

BODY LOTION

HAIR BRUSHING

HOT SHOWER

TICKLE

BATHTUB SOAK

SHOULDER MASSAGE

WARM BLANKET

DESCRIBE THE PHYSICAL TREATS THAT YOUR BODY LOVES.

Give yourself (or ask for one) now!

WHO'S THE FRIEND THAT YOU LAUGH TO TEARS WITH?

....

DESCRIBE YOUR LAST LOL MOMENT WITH THEM.

VISUALIZATION VACATION!

Sit comfortably, close your eyes, and take a soothing breath. In your mind, picture a place you've always wanted to go for a vacation. Imagine yourself there now on an all-expense-paid trip. Take your time and imagine in detail: how it feels to be there, what it looks like around you, what amazing activity you're doing, and who's there with you that you're so happy to share this with. Keep adding details to this visualization vacation for as long as you want.

DESCRIBE IT HERE.

Spill your sadness here . . .

Celebrate the relief here . . .

CIRCLE YOUR FAVORITE FLAVORS

grape
salty
cheddar
ginger
cinnamon
cola
sweet
coconut
sour
sweet-cream
watermelon
honey-mustard
bitter
strawberry

pickle
savory
pistachio
cherry
melon
pumpkin
chocolate
spicy
basil
ranch
BBQ
licorice
root-beer
nutmeg

pecan
apple
mint
caramel
lime
pepper
almond

(And add any more of your own.)

smoky

raspberry

sharp

egg

molasses

coffee

mocha

orange

chamomile

dill

chili

lavender

peanut

vanilla

maple

parmesan

bacon

lemon

★ Put stars by the TOP 5. ★

Find at least one of these for yourself now—or soon! Describe its deliciousness.

WATCH A "CUTEST" VIDEO RIGHT NOW AND WRITE ABOUT WHAT MAKES YOU SMILE.

PUPPIES?

Kittens?

Babies?

Or?

Without any planning or forethought

doodle some NOTES or PICTURES or IDEAS or SCRIBBLES

all over this page about WHAT MAKES YOU FEEL JOY.

YOU'VE BEEN NAMED:

How do you change the school to bring every student joy?

Which classes or activities do you eliminate?

What new classes and activities do you bring in?

What time does school start and stop?

How long is lunch?

What's served in the cafeteria?

What else?
Make your OWN RULES that make it a joy-filled day for everyone!

Imagine your **SADNESS** as a creature.
Draw it here.

Then write a bold
"GOODBYE"
across this page.

Imagine your **JOY** as another creature.
Draw it here.

Then write a warm **"HELLO!"** and **WELCOME!"** across this page.

LOOK FOR YOUR "*glimmers*" TODAY!

(Anything at all that makes you smile or triggers your joy!)

RECORD THEM ALL HERE:

Who do you love to snuggle with?

(Draw them or tape their picture here.)

Describe the **joy** of this connection.

1 **INSIDE SQUARE 1:** Write 3 words about your sadness here and leave the cracks open so the sadness can leak out.

2 **INSIDE SQUARE 2:** Color this space with a sad color. Leave the cracks open so the sadness can leak out.

3 **INSIDE SQUARE 3:** Write 6 words about something you are grateful for here. Leave the cracks open so the sadness can leak out.

4 **INSIDE SQUARE 4:** Color this space with happy colors. Leave the cracks open so the sadness can leak out.

5 **ON THE OUTSIDE:** Color the rest of the space on the page with joyful colors. Show the sadness leaking out of the center and being overcome by the joy.

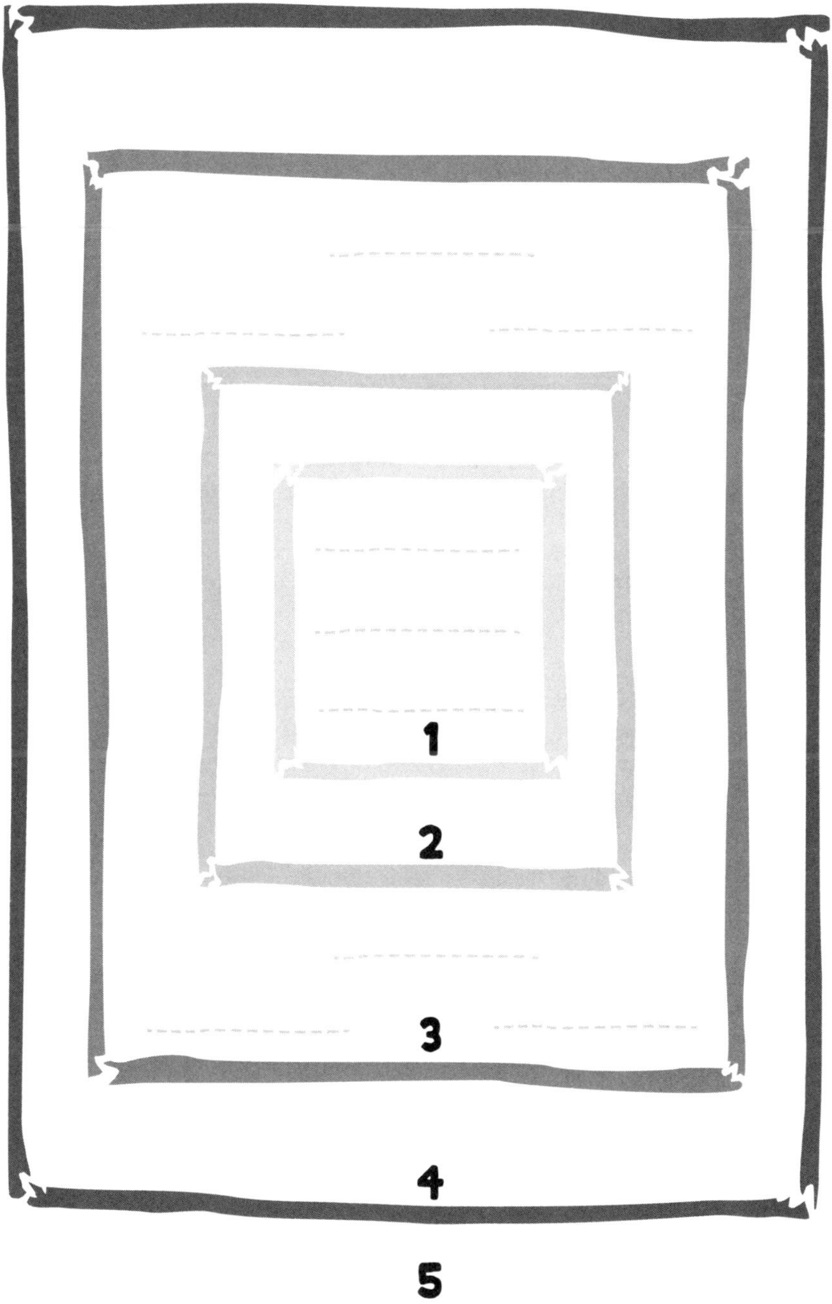
1
2
3
4
5

Sit quietly and comfortably.

Close your eyes or lower your gaze.

Imagine that you are joy.

Breathe in your lightness and sparkle;
follow it as it flows through
every part of your body and
fills every cell of your being.

Embrace this bliss.

Let your whole body smile.

Once you have found joy and beauty within, the whole world becomes infused with joy and beauty.

—PANDIT RAJMANI TIGUNAIT

Use lines or color to express your inner joy

EXPLORE YOUR **FIVE SENSES OF JOY**

WHAT DO YOU **LOVE** TO . . .

LOOK AT?

LISTEN TO?

TASTE?

SMELL?

FEEL ON YOUR SKIN?

OMG! YOU JUST GOT THE

BEST NEWS EVER!

YOU CAN HARDLY BELIEVE IT! TELL THE DETAILS HERE:

Fill in this **TIMELINE** with the highlight reel scenes from your life . . .

INCLUDE EVERYTHING YOU CAN REMEMBER THAT'S BROUGHT YOU JOY, **BIG** AND SMALL.

EARLIEST MEMORY OF JOY

MOST RECENT
MEMORY OF JOY

WRITE A LETTER TO YOUR SADNESS,
LETTING IT KNOW THAT YOU ACCEPT IT AND RESPECT IT,
--- BUT ---
YOU'RE NOT GOING TO LET IT RUIN YOUR LIFE.

Dear Sadness,

Yours truly,

CREATE A JOY TATTOO

Where would you put it?

Describe or list anything and everything you could do just for your own COMFORT and ENJOYMENT.

Choose one and do it now!

"SELF-CARE"

yourself into a state of contentment and bliss!

OUTSIDE!

CIRCLE ~ STAR ~ DOODLE YOUR FAVORITES.

Add any more that you need.

SAND

grass

trees

WAVES

breezes

CLIFFS

SUN

DEER

STONES

stars

POND

clouds

RAIN

snow

leaves

blossoms

shells

butterflies

TRAILS

dirt

PEBBLES

BOULDERS

meadow

sea glass

DEW

canyons

birds

RIVER

MOON

wildflowers

DESERT

MOUNTAIN PEAKS

wind

CAMPGROUND

ocean

buds

feathers

wind chimes

orchards

WHITEWATER RAPIDS

rays of sun

NESTS

PUDDLES

frost

ROCKS

FROGS

Sadness can be selfish and want *ALL* your attention.

BUT SADNESS

DOES NOT

OWN YOU.

Write a list of rules for your sadness to remind it that you are the boss. →

For example...

- ✓ You may not overwhelm me.
- ✓ You may not ruin my day.
- ✓ You may not come to the movies with me.
- ✓ You may only make me cry once a day.

DESCRIBE WHAT YOU'D LIKE TO SEE WHEN YOU

FIRST OPEN YOUR EYES IN THE MORNING

WHAT WOULD FILL YOU WITH JOY?

(Details please!)

Doing any kind of physical exercise raises the endorphin (FEEL-GOOD chemical) levels in our brain.

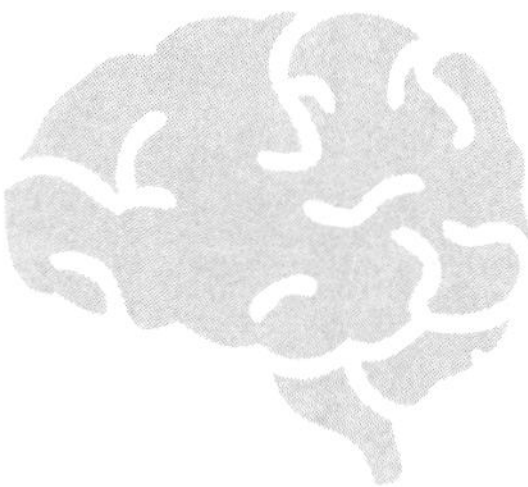

DRAW OR DESCRIBE YOUR FAVORITE WAY TO GET MOVING—

THEN DO IT!

(If you can't do it right now, take a walk or a deep-stretch break.)

✱ Fill in these GOLD MEDALS with any achievements you're proud of.

(Finished grade school? Stuck out something hard? Been a good friend? Baked a cake? Joined a club?)

Decorate those that bring you the most joy.

What music starts your . . .

TOES TAPPING?

MOUTH SMILING?

eyes brightening?

body dancing?

Write your Joy Songs Playlist here:

My Playlist

JOY SONGS

1 ______________________________

2 ______________________________

3 ______________________________

4 ______________________________

5

6

7

8

9

10

11

12

13

14

15

Write about your sadness in the third person.

For example: "She was feeling sad because . . ." or
"He could feel the sadness in his chest . . ." or
"The sadness seemed to begin whenever they thought about . . ."

Let yourself observe
and feel compassion for
the person you're
describing without taking
on their sorrow.

CREATE AN AMAZING **FRIEND EVENT!**

CONCERT? PARTY? BONFIRE?

DANCE? DAY AT THE WATER PARK?

GIVE **ALL** THE DETAILS

WHO

What

When

Where

What else?

FILL THIS PAGE WITH COLORS OF JOY!

Write a dialogue with your SADNESS.

Sadness

Me

Sadness

Me

Sadness

Me

Write a dialogue with your JOY.

Joy

Me

Joy

Me

Joy

Me

CREATE A JOLLIDAY!

(A holiday where everyone celebrates joy!)

- WHAT TIME OF YEAR WOULD IT BE?
- WHAT DATE?
- OFFICIAL NAME?
- HOW WOULD PEOPLE CELEBRATE?
- ACTIVITIES?

★ FOODS?

★ GAMES?

★ COLORS?

★ SYMBOLS, LOGOS, OR FLAGS?

★ WOULD THERE BE GIFT GIVING?

★ WHAT WOULD YOU LIKE THE VERY BEST ABOUT THIS DAY?

EMBRACE SILLINESS!

Enjoy these REAL words and
then make up some of your own.

bumfuzzle *(to confuse someone)*

erf *(a plot of land)*

MELDROP *(drop of mucus)*

smicker *(to look amorously at someone)*

biblioklept *(person who steals books)*

finifugal *(someone afraid of finishing things)*

SMAZE *(combination of smoke and haze)*

How about a word for:

Fear of taco sauce?

Sleeping with your foot in your mouth?

A banana peel worn as a bandana?

Gum stuck under a desk?

Person addicted to sauerkraut?

When you forget to study for a test
but get a perfect score?

The last chip in the bag?

(Add more of your own . . .)

Are you holding back tears?

Cry yourself a river here!

Fill it with all your sadness.

Then draw yourself in a lifeboat named "Hope."

Feel yourself being saved!

JOY is the glitter and confetti of life.

Decorate this page with any kind of glitter or confetti (homemade is fine!) in colors and designs that you love.

RESEARCH

SHOWS THAT

GIVING

TO OTHERS

CAN TRIGGER

OUR BRAIN'S

PLEASURE

CENTERS.

Whose face could you LIGHT UP right now?

Text,

call,

visit,

hug,

email,

post,

meme,

or - ?

Do it . . .

Sadness is a normal reaction to loss.

a job — confidence — your reputation — time — a sense of purpose — innocence — personal belongings — part of yourself — or? Write or draw it out.

Have you lost anything recently? — an opportunity — a relationship — a hope — a dream — good health — a loved one — a game — a good grade — your childhood — trust — comfort — faith — positivity —

ONCE YOU START **PRACTICING JOY,**

IT WILL **ATTRACT** MORE!

WHAT COULD YOU DO EVERY MORNING . . .

EVERY EVENING . . .

EVERY MONTH . . .

EVERY YEAR . . .

EVERY WEEKEND . . .

THAT WILL HELP JOY FIND ITS WAY TO YOU?

"The more light you allow within you, the brighter the world you live in will be."

—SHAKTI GAWAIN

1. TOSS YOUR SAD THOUGHTS ALL OVER THESE PAGES.
2. TAPE THE PAGES SHUT.
3. TEAR THEM OUT AND DESTROY THEM!

What do you soooo look forward to —just can't wait until it happens?

Describe this joy here . . .

What we feed grows stronger.

Help your joy thrive by feeding it sunny thoughts.

SOMETHING GOOD IS RIGHT AROUND THE CORNER

IT'S A BEAUTIFUL DAY

SUNNY THOUGHTS MAKE ME SMILE

IMAGINE IT'S FIVE YEARS FROM NOW.

Draw or describe a scene from what you'd like your Ideal Life to be—no restrictions!

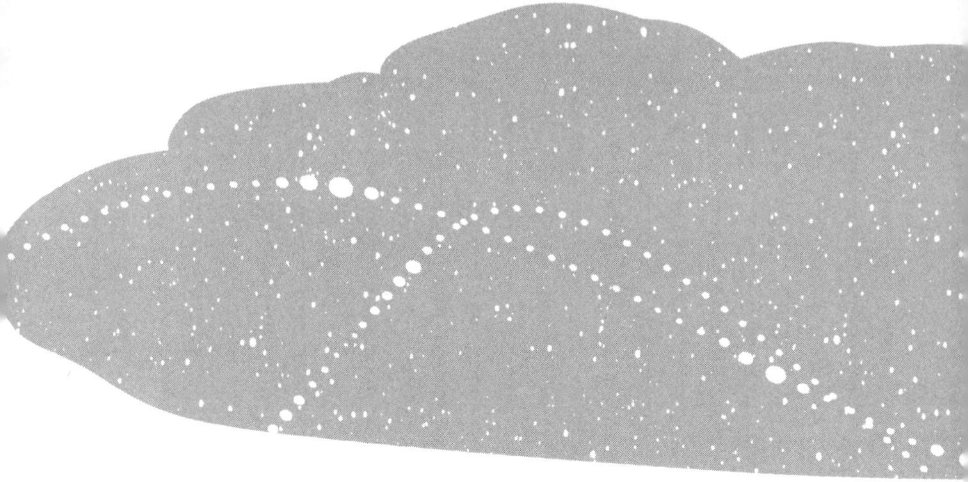

Insert BRIGHT COLORS of joy into these dark clouds.

(Use whatever medium or materials feel good to you!)

Circle the JOY GLIMMERS that you love . . .

SUNLIGHT SPARKLES ON THE WATER

FIRST NEW GREEN OF SPRING

SOFT BREEZE ON YOUR FACE

SOUND OF WIND CHIMES

LOOKING INTO THE EYES OF SOMEONE YOU LOVE

A SMALL CHILD GIVING YOU A HUG

BEING APPRECIATED

BEING IN THE CREATIVE FLOW

HEARING FROM A FRIEND YOU'D LOST TOUCH WITH

DRESSING UP FOR HALLOWEEN

A ROMANTIC MOMENT

MOONLIGHT ON SNOW

FINDING MONEY IN YOUR POCKET

OPENING A PRESENT THAT KNOCKS YOU OVER

JUMPING IN THE POOL ON THE HOTTEST DAY

WRITE MORE OF YOUR OWN . . .

WRITE OR DRAW EVERYTHING YOU VALUE MOST IN THIS SAFE.

Possessions? Friends? Health? Experiences? Laughter? Money? Achievements? Honesty? Independence? Free Time? Add your own!

NUMBER THEM IN ORDER OF IMPORTANCE.

CHOOSE ONE OR TWO TO DESCRIBE IN DETAIL.

HOW DO THEY BRING YOU JOY?

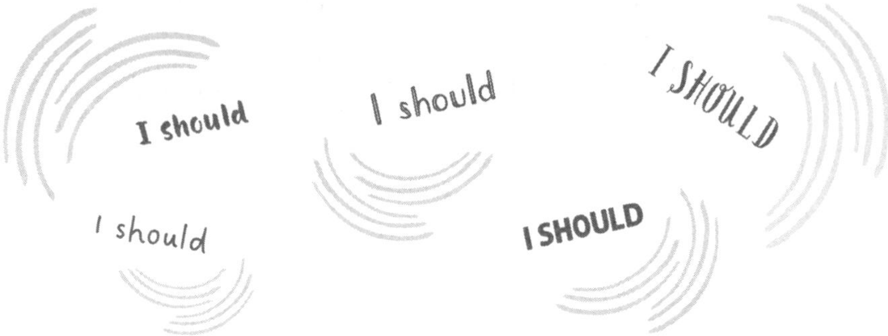

WHAT "SHOULDS" HAUNT YOU?

LEAVE THEM HERE.

WHAT BRINGS YOU DELIGHT, MAGIC, OR WINGS TO SOAR?

DESCRIBE AND CELEBRATE THESE HERE.

You Won!!!

Describe the joy here
(and what you won.)

5:00

COMPARTMENTALIZE.

(DWELL ON YOUR SADNESS FOR LIMITED AMOUNTS OF TIME.)

1. Set a timer for five minutes.
2. Let yourself feel the sadness within you and through you.
3. Write all about it here.

When the bell goes off, close the sadness compartment and move on until next time.

What's your passion?

PAINTING . . .

SKIING . . .

PLAYING GUITAR . . .

SWIMMING . . .

PROGRAMMING . . .

SCULPTING . . .

SINGING . . .

BASKETBALL . . .

READING . . .

GAMING . . .

BOWLING . . .

OR . . . ?

DESCRIBE WHAT IT'S LIKE
WHEN YOU'RE

IN THE ZONE.

GO THERE NOW IF YOU CAN.

Draw or describe your BIGGEST burden.

Then describe how it would feel to LET IT GO!

Comparison is the thief of joy.

Who do you compare yourself to?

How can you appreciate your authentic self and take back your joy?

EVERYDAY MIRACLES that are so common we take them for granted: get a paper cut and it heals ... a tiny pup grows into a St. Bernard ... wake up in the morning ... sunrise—doesn't miss a day ... seasons change—haven't missed a year ... eat pizza/fries/apples and they become our eyes/skin/fingernails/limbs

WHAT MIRACLES
IN YOUR LIFE

BRING YOU JOY?

FINISH THESE LAUGH LIMERICKS IN WHATEVER WAY MAKES YOU SMILE

There once was a zombie from Phoenix . . .

A frog by the name of Ned . . .

Last night at the party at Joe's . . .

The thing about raspberry clams . . .

When Joker and Batman went riding . . .

There once was a boy named Stu
who kept ice cream cones in his shoe
When asked if they squished
He said, "Yes, but theyre delish!
So there's nothing that I'd rather do!"

List any irrational

"ALL-OR-NOTHING THOUGHTS"

that fuel your sadness.

(For example, "There's nothing good about me." "I always mess up." "No one cares.")

Explain the **TRUE STORY** here.

(For example, "Well, actually here's something good about me . . ." "Here's a time I did not mess up and did great . . ." "This is someone who cares about me, even if I forget this sometimes . . .")

CONFIDENT BODY LANGUAGE TELLS YOUR BRAIN YOU'RE HAPPY EVEN IF YOU'RE NOT!

1.

Try this:
Focus your thoughts on something sad and describe how your body responds.

2.

Then try this:
Sit or stand up tall, pull your shoulders back, open your arms wide, look up, and smile to the sky.

Write or draw about this experiment.

TAPE OR DRAW A PICTURE OF YOURSELF AS A **CHILD** IN THIS FRAME.

Fill in the surrounding space with words or pictures of whatever brought you joy as a little kid.

(Blowing bubbles? Making slime? Watching cartoons? Being tickled? Jumping into a pool? Water balloons? Eating a popsicle?)

REMEMBER THIS HAPPINESS!

These FORTUNE COOKIES contain the very messages you want to read to bring you joy. **What do they say?**

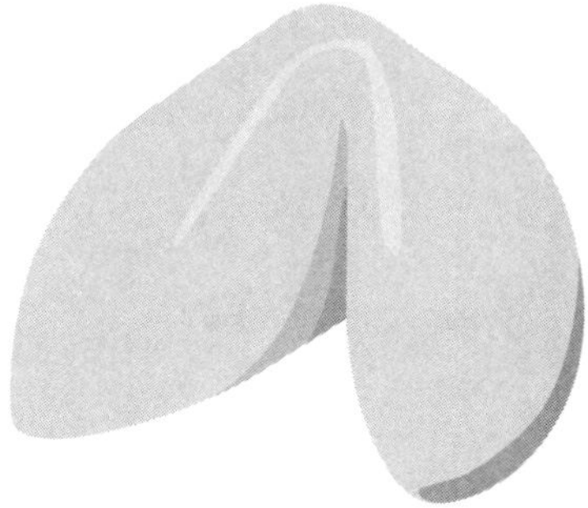

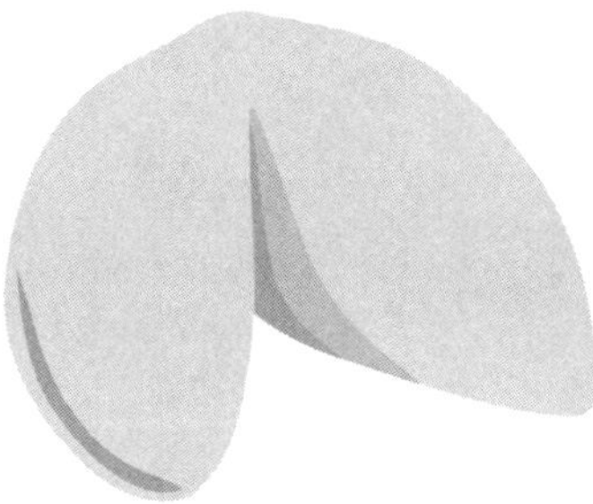

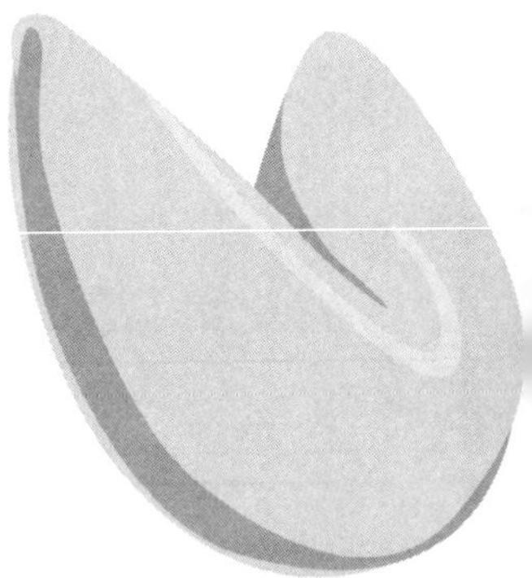

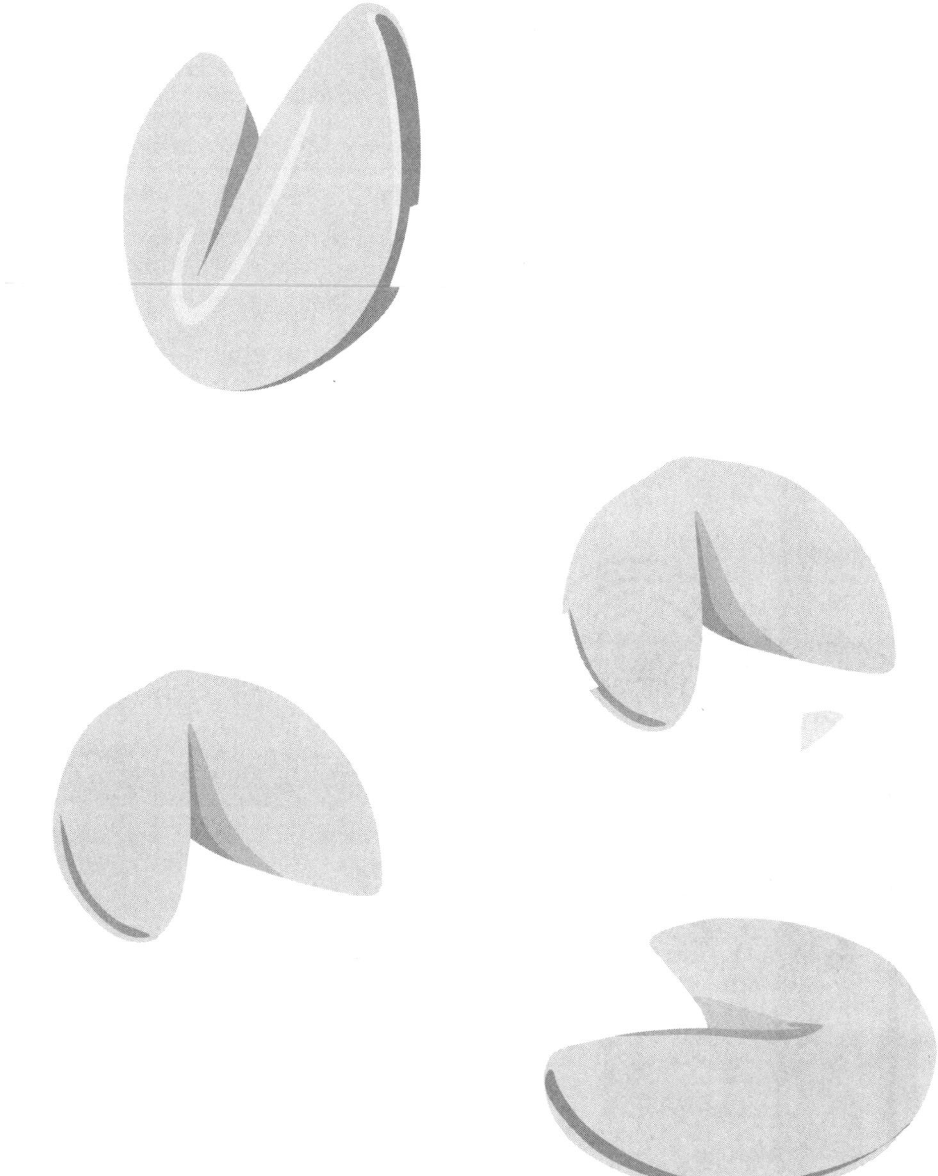

COLLAGE THESE PAGES WITH **ANYTHING** THAT BRINGS YOU **JOY!** PHOTOS, MEMES, QUOTES, COLORS, STICKERS, MEMORIES, DREAMS, FABRIC . . . OR ?

You've been given a free week in a LUXURY VACATION HOUSE with all your friends and an unlimited budget!

Describe how this **Joy Time** plays out...

Where are you? / Who's there? / What's to eat? / Swimming pool?

Pool table? / Big screens? / Dance floor? / Great views?

7 steps

1 Close your eyes and notice where you feel sadness in your body.

2 Map it here.

3 Describe the physical sensation.

4 Accept. It's OK to feel this!

5 Close your eyes again and imagine "unhooking" the sadness from where it's caught within you.

6 Picture it rising up and drifting away. Stay with this image until it's all released.

7 Draw a new you, with the sadness gone.

WOULD YOU RATHER . . .

(HIGHLIGHT YOUR ANSWERS!)

Swim in a pool of chocolate pudding or strawberry ice cream?

Buy all used underwear or all used toothbrushes?

Be invisible or able to fly?

Always have an annoying song stuck in your head or an itch that you can't reach?

Wake up naked in a forest 5 miles from home or in your underwear at school?

Have a permanent unibrow or no eyebrows at all?

Always cough confetti or always burp bubbles?

See only in black and white or glow in the dark?

Get tickled for an hour straight
or listen to an annoying laugh for a whole day?

Be totally hairless
or covered in hair head to toe?

Sweat honey
or hot sauce?

Only crawl on all fours
or only walk backwards?

Be able to talk to animals
or control the weather?

Eat a raw potato
or a whole lemon?

Own a car that can fly
or go underwater?

Have a bucket stuck on your head
or cement block stuck on your foot?

Have to wear a clown wig
or clown nose for the rest of your life?

DESIGN YOUR JOYRIDE . . .

WHAT DOES IT LOOK LIKE?

COLOR?

STYLE?

DASHBOARD?

SEATS?

ACCESSORIES?

WHERE WOULD YOU GO??

WHEN YOUR

THOUGHTS MOVE TO

FEARS OR UNKNOWNS

AND CREATE SADNESS,

COME BACK TO THE

PRESENT MOMENT.

FOCUS ON EVERYTHING
THAT IS OK RIGHT NOW.

(Are you breathing? Is there hope? Will you have another meal?)

WRITE YOUR COMFORT LIST HERE.

ALPHA-BLISS!

From Apple-pie-with-ice-cream to Zipline-over-a-lake...

WRITE ANYTHING THAT MAKES YOU HAPPY STARTING WITH EACH LETTER OF THE ALPHABET.

A ______________________________

B ______________________________

C ______________________________

D ______________________________

E ______________________________

F ______________________________

G ______________________________

H ______________________________

I ______________________________

J ______________________________

K ______________________________

L

M

N

O

P

Q

R

S

T

U

V

W

X

Y

Z

PLAY "HIDDEN JOYS"

TODAY.

Search for bits of JOY hidden in the busyness of your activities and tasks and interactions. Is there something to appreciate in everything you encounter? The more you look, the more you'll find!

LIST OR DESCRIBE THEM HERE.

WHAT'S THE WEATHER RIGHT NOW

AND HOW CAN YOU EN-JOY IT?

Raining? Jump in puddles! Sunny? Lie on the earth and watch clouds! Windy?

Let your hair blow! Snowing? Catch flakes on your tongue! Clear night? Wish on stars! Or - ?

* DRAW OR WRITE ABOUT WHAT FELT GOOD.

IT'S **OPEN MIC NIGHT** ~ AND YOU'RE A POPULAR STAND-UP COMIC!

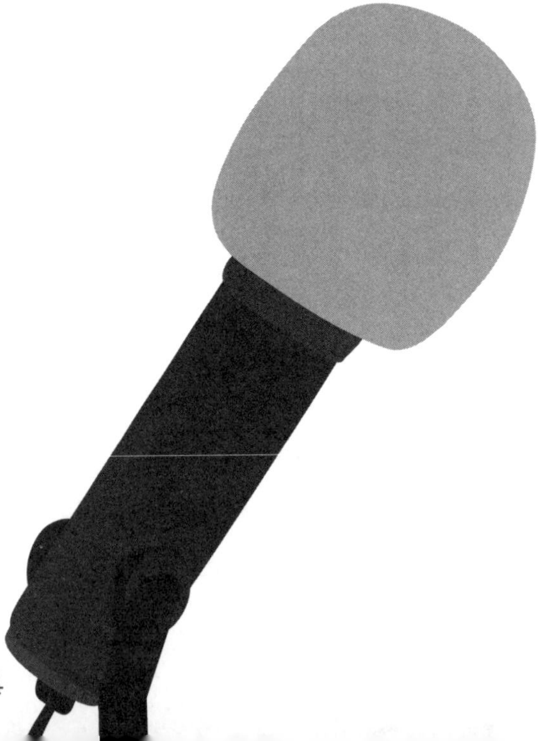

WRITE A COMEDY SCRIPT ABOUT YOUR SAD SITUATION, HIGHLIGHTING THE TWISTS AND TURNS THAT WILL MAKE YOUR AUDIENCE LAUGH OUT LOUD.

> The three grand essentials
> of happiness are:
> something to do,
> someone to love, and
> something to hope for.
>
> - GEORGE BURNAP

DESCRIBE ANY **GRAND ESSENTIALS** THAT BRING HAPPINESS TO YOUR LIFE . . .

Spend the next 15-30 minutes **TAKING PICTURES** of anything that brings you joy.

Walk around your house, room, school, neighborhood, yard, or wherever you are and record anything that trips your smile!

- Birds in flight?
- Funny bug?
- Poster?
- Person?
- Animal?
- Favorite food?
- Act of love?

LIST OR DESCRIBE YOUR FINDS HERE.

Then file the pics in a **JOY** folder or album. View them when you need a mood boost!

What makes the

HOPE LIGHT SHINE

at the end of your dark tunnel?

Write about it here.

WHAT TO DO NEXT →

SOME IDEAS ON HOW TO CONTINUE GETTING ----------

1. Remember, it's an ongoing journey. Just like breathing and eating—as long as we're alive we're never done. So don't beat yourself up if you think you've got sadness licked and then you feel it coming around again. It doesn't work that way! The goal isn't to eliminate sadness, it's to find peace with it. Move through the moments of sadness and celebrate the moments of joy!

2. Flip back through the pages of this journal and look for the prompts that worked best for you.

★ List your TOP 5 FOR MANAGING SADNESS here:

1 ________________ page# ______

2 ________________ page# ______

3 ________________ page# ______

4 ________________ page# ______

5 ________________ page# ______

★ List your TOP 5 FOR FINDING JOY here:

1 ________________ page# ______

2 ________________ page# ______

3 ________________ page# ______

4 ________________ page# ______

5 ________________ page# ______

Do you notice any patterns? Write your observations here:

3. Use the info in #2 to guide you forward. Notice what helps you the most and repeat that when you can. Try variations on those themes! Create your own prompts that can help you release sadness and find joy. Try one here:

MY OWN PROMPT:

4. Be kind to yourself! As was established in the introduction, you are most likely a human being living on the planet Earth. It's an amazing place! But not without its challenges. So, treat yourself with compassion as you travel along. This attitude works the best for dealing with sadness and coming back to joy. Be a caring travel companion for yourself and you'll create a much happier life!

NOTE TO PARENTS, PROFESSIONALS, AND ANYONE CARING FOR A TEEN

Find Your Joy Here offers over 80 journaling prompts designed specifically to help teens recognize, accept, and release sadness and depression and shift to feelings of happiness and joy. Working with this material will help create neural patterns that assist the brain in moving away from sadness more readily. Completing the prompts helps readers practice making this shift *in the moment* as well as over time. These creative, engaging, and clinically-based prompts are grounded in the principles of Cognitive Behavioral Therapy, as well as Dialectical Behavioral Therapy, Mindfulness-Based Therapies, and Neuroscience.

This journal can be used by a teen on their own, or as an adjunct to counseling or psychotherapy. It lends itself both to individual and group settings and can help the average adolescent as well as the hard-to-reach teen and those uncomfortable with traditional talk therapy.

Where direct questioning and exploration might feel threatening, journaling prompts are more subtle and can bypass defenses. When used at times of sadness or depression, the journal can help the teen to interrupt the habitual downward spiraling thought cycle, decrease negativity, and shift to a happier experience. The prompts are designed to help teens start dismantling negative thought patterns and building new neural pathways for managing sad feelings through cognitive restructuring, visualization, meditation, mind-body awareness, self-soothing, and self-expression. These creative prompts help teens raise their self-awareness of what triggers both their sadness and happiness and helps develop confidence in their ability to move from one to the other while maintaining comfort with the process.

For a clinical guide *to using this book specifically, and journaling as an adjunct to therapy in general, please visit http://www.lisamschabooks.com. Alternatively, you can visit http://www.newharbinger.com/56197 and follow the instructions there to register your book and download the companion guide.*

Acknowledgments

My heartfelt thank yous to:

Tesilya Hanauer and Madison Davis again and again for their confidence in and celebration of my writing.

Amy Shoup and Sara Christian for weaving their design magic around my words.

Amy Blue, my expert research librarian, who generously lends her time and energy to these journals.

Everyone on the New Harbinger staff who contributes to the creation of these books and helps the readers grow and heal.

And thank you to all of those humans ~ family, friends, therapists, professors, teachers, and unbeknownst guides who have escorted me along my own journey and made the content of this book possible.

Lisa M. Schab, LCSW, is a practicing psychotherapist in the greater Chicago, IL, area; and author of twenty-four self-help books, including *The Anxiety Workbook for Teens*, *The Self-Esteem Workbook for Teens*, and the teen guided journals, *Put Your Worries Here*, *Put Your Feelings Here*, and *Find Your Self-Love Here*.

Schab has been interviewed as an expert on Milwaukee television stations WTMJ-TV and WISN-TV, and by *The New York Times*, *Scholastic Choices* magazine, *Teen Vogue*, *Psych Central*, and Kate Shannon's *Creative Therapy Umbrella* podcast. Schab has authored regular mental health columns for *Chicago Parent Magazine* and *The Sun* newspapers. She is a member of the National Association of Social Workers (NASW) and the Society of Children's Book Writers and Illustrators (SCBWI).